Acknowledgments

7263695

We are indebted to a number of naturalists and photographers for assistance in the preparation of this book. Some of their names are mentioned in the text but we would like to thank Dr. A. G. Lyne in particular for his reading of the final text.

Thanks are also due to the scientists and other officers of the National Parks and Wildlife Service of New South Wales; the Primary Industries Department of Queensland; and the Fisheries and Wildlife Division of Victoria. The Australian Information Service was of great help with regard to photographs.

Photo Credits: Australian Information Service: pp. 10, 32, 49, 60, 61, 66, 70-71, 72, 73, 75; J. Brownlie: pp. 4, 24; H. Frauca: pp. 27, 34, 63; G. Lewis: pp. 3, 13, 14, 19, 21, 39, 43, 47, 55; A. G. Lyne: pp. 8, 16, 56, 58; W. Sutherland: pp. 30, 51; M. Wentworth: p. 41; Western Australian Government Tourist Bureau: p. 48; Eric Worrell: p. 7. Photographs not credited are by Vincent Serventy.

Dutton-Sunrise, Inc., a subsidiary of E. P. Dutton & Co., Inc.

Published simultaneously in Canada by Clarke, Irwin & Company Limited, Toronto and Vancouver

ISBN: 0-87690-195-X

Library of Congress Cataloging in Publication Data

Serventy, Vincent.
  The koala.

  (A Sunrise book)
  1. Koalas. I. Serventy, Carol, joint author.
II. Title.
QL737.M38S45   599′.2   75-11827
Printed and bound in Spain by
Novograph, S. A., and Roner, S. A.
D. L.: M. 30.958-1975.

CONTENTS

Eating is a serious business, and even the unexpected intrusion of a photographer does not interrupt the meal.

1. THE KOALA IN TIME

Love at first sight is most people's reaction to seeing a live koala clinging to an Australian gum tree. Here is the teddy bear of childhood miraculously come to life. With what solemnity the koala stares down at this huge human being! Its air of gravity and sagacity is irresistible.

Whether it is just surveying the bushland scene or moving with deliberation from one branch to another in search of food or a more comfortable sleeping place, the koala prefers to take things quietly and with decorum. If it feels hungry, it pulls a spray of gum leaves toward its mouth. No, the koala decides, the leaves look a trifle tough. It tries another spray. Just right. Still with the same supreme gravity the koala begins eating, staring unblinkingly at you while the green scimitar-shaped eucalypt leaves disappear between its munching jaws.

This is the koala, the Australian marsupial which in the few hundred years since its discovery in 1798 has become better and better known around the world, until today it shares with the panda the title of the world's best-loved animal.

Australia has been described as a huge ark, a giant lifeboat, cut off from contact with the rest of the world and carrying with it a group of unique creatures saved from competition from—and probably extinction by—more efficient and aggressive animals. For sixty million years this ark has been isolated from most other animals and plants, except for those occasional invaders which, by flying, or by drifting on rafts of tree trunks, managed to cross the ocean barriers and reach this continent.

In recent years there has been a gradual acceptance of the idea that

After its daytime sleep a koala wakes in the afternoon to begin a night of feeding in the tree tops. The large ears distinguish the koalas found in southern Australia from those living in the hotter northern areas.

continents drift and that those that were once linked have moved away from each other. Australia, for example, was once closely linked with South America, South Africa, India, and Antarctica. This grouping broke apart some one hundred and eighty million years ago. Gradually Australia broke land link after land link, finally parting company with Antarctica about forty-five million years ago as it moved away to the northeast.

How does the koala fit into this geological story? As a fur-bearing warm-blooded animal whose young are fed on milk, it is a mammal, one of the great group of animals which first appeared when the giant reptiles dominated the earth some two hundred million years ago. Warm-blooded mammals and warm-blooded birds gradually increased in numbers due to the fact that they could control their body temperatures and so remain active in cold as well as warm conditions. They could feed at any time of the day or night and even penetrate the regions of ice and snow barred to the reptiles.

6

High above the ground in the fork of a tree the sleeping animal is safe from most enemies.

About sixty-five million years ago the mammals began their greatest period of expansion. One strange branch, the egg-laying mammals, either evolved independently or branched off from the mainstream of evolution. Scientists do not even know where these egg layers, the platypus and the echidna, first appeared. They are found today only in the Australian region and therefore remain another mammal mystery of this southern continent.

An equally extraordinary group of mammals are the marsupials, creatures whose young, when born, are extremely tiny, in fact in an embryonic state, and need to be sheltered in a pouch developed on the mother's belly. Here the youngster feeds on milk until it is large enough to face the outside world. A six-foot-high kangaroo is born only about an inch in length and only about one thirty-thousandth the weight of the mother. Compare this with a human baby, perhaps a sixteenth of the weight of the mother, or a baby calf or pony, which a few hours after its birth is able to run alongside its mother!

Newborn marsupial babies are extraordinarily small. This baby kangaroo about the size of a human fingernail will grow to six feet.

Where did the marsupials come from? That is still a mystery, but most authorities on these Australian marsupials think that they probably reached Australia by island-hopping from South America into Antarctica, then into Australia, between eighty million and one hundred and twenty million years ago. Today some marsupials still live in the Americas—the Virginia opossum in the North, and some seventy species in Central and South America.

The Australian marsupials were fortunate in that they had a continent empty of mammal competition. As Australia slowly drifted north, they evolved into a vast array of different forms. Some were grass eaters; some moved into the trees and fed on leaves; others were flesh eaters.

Possibly bats had already reached Australia, so no flying marsupials ever evolved, though gliding marsupials developed in the forests. No Australian marsupial took to the water, although there is an aquatic marsupial in South America. The competition of the platypus may have stopped them. As Australia drifted closer to Asia, more placental mammals island-hopped into the north of the continent. These were the native rats and mice, as well as more bats. Though Australia is often thought of as a place of marsupials, since these dominate the scene, the placental rats, mice, and bats almost equal them in the number of different kinds which live on the continent.

Today Australia has two of the five known species of the egg-laying mammals or monotremes in the world; the other three are found close by in New Guinea. Of the 240 species of marsupials in the world, Australia has 120, and of the 3400 world placentals, Australia has 110. This means that Australia has about 7 per cent of the world's mammals, a figure roughly similar to that for other groups of animals.

Yet today Australia, so far as mammals are concerned, is a continent that has fallen on hard times. Australia was once a much wetter land, with lush forests. Among the grazing animals were giant kangaroos, some nine feet tall, giant wombatlike animals as big as a hippopotamus, and flesh-eating marsupial lions, much larger than the Tasmanian tiger which perhaps still survives in some remote forests of Tasmania. Today these giants are known only as fossils, destroyed possibly by the drying out of the continent in an arid period which turned the central two-thirds of it into a near desert.

An even more destructive force reached Australia, probably also island-hopping in from the north. This was aboriginal man, who came to Australia possibly as long ago as fifty thousand years and certainly as long ago as thirty thousand years. In his hunger for meat he most probably wiped out some of the giants among the marsupials.

Although fire was always present in older Australia, started by lightning

9

Near the rivers which wind through the eucalypt or gumtree forests of eastern Australia live the platypus, the strange egglaying mammal found only in the Australian region.

strikes and raging across the bushland, man used fire as a hunting weapon, and soon Australia became a land filled with smoke. Early explorers commented on the sight of smoke seen from offshore. By the time the first white settlers arrived, all the native animals and plants had become adjusted to hunting man. Those that could not survive the impact of fire, the spear, and later the hunting dog of the aboriginal—the dingo—died out.

Then came agricultural man, and the native animals faced even greater disasters. At least six marsupials and probably seven have become extinct, and another 40 per cent are on the verge of extinction. This once well-filled Australian ark has lost some of its fascinating cargo.

Will the koala go the way of the toolache wallaby, the brown hare wallaby, and the Tasmanian tiger, or has it been saved in the nick of time?

Fortunately the answer is yes, with conservation efforts being vigorously implemented, as outlined in Chapter 6. Now we turn to the biology of the koala, its place among the marsupials, and its intriguing life history.

On the forest floor lives the echidna, also known as the spiny anteater. Like the platypus, the echidna is an egglaying mammal.

2. A TREE-CLIMBING WOMBAT?

At the time of the first settlement in New South Wales in 1788, the coastal areas around Sydney had so few koalas that the discovery of the koala by the white settlers was delayed for ten years.

John Price, a young man working for John Hunter, the governor of the colony at the time, told of the first discovery in 1798. Price's guide and assistant was an ex-convict named James Wilson who had lived among the local aborigines and learned something of survival in the Australian bush. He found "an animal which the natives call a cullawine which much resembles the sloths in America." This was the koala. John Price also shot the first Australian "pheasant"—the beautiful bird known today as the superb lyrebird.

A few years later another explorer described "portions of a monkey" brought in by the natives, whose name for it was "colo." The first live animal was then caught, and the news was sent home to Great Britain.

The English, already amazed at the story of the giant kangaroo, were delighted with this oddity, an animal described in an 1803 newspaper account as "this creature somewhat larger than a wombat . . . the graveness of its visage . . . would seem to indicate a more than ordinary portion of animal sagacity. . . . The surviving pup generally clings to the back of the mother or is caressed with a serenity that appears characteristic; it has a false belly . . . its food consists solely of gum leaves, in the choice of which it is excessively nice."

So, more than a hundred and fifty years ago the reporter highlighted the aspects of the koala that fascinate us to this day. The "false belly" is the

A gray kangaroo doe and her baby, which lives for many months in the mother's snug pouch where it feeds on milk.

After about six months in the safety of the pouch the baby koala moves onto the mother's back.

characteristic pouch of the marsupial group, and the "excessively nice" choice of gum leaves was not a gastronomical idiosyncrasy, but a matter of life or death for the animal, since at certain times of the year gum leaves may be poisonous.

Peter Cunningham, another writer of those early years, in *Two Years in New South Wales* described some marsupials, including the koala, in the following words:

> The opossums and squirrels are good eating having much the taste and flavour of rabbit but required to be soaked in water some time previously to take away the strong aromatic odour of the gumtree leaves on which they feed. The bandicoot tastes somewhat like a suckling-pig and makes a delicious dish with a well-prepared pudding in its belly. . . . Our coola (sloth or native bear) is about the size of an ordinary poodle dog wth shaggy, dirty coloured fur, no tail and claws like a bear, of which it forms a tolerable miniature. It climbs trees readily and feeds upon their leaves, getting very fat . . . the flesh being much esteemed by the natives.

A variety of common names was given to this engaging marsupial. Native monkey, native sloth, wombat, colo, native bear, cullawine, and koala were the most common. Gradually all but two were dropped, koala and koala bear. "Koala" is a native term and was said to mean the "animal that does not drink," though the ability to go for long periods without water is not uncommon in animals, particularly Australian ones, living in a dry country. Koalas do at times drink some water.

The name "koala bear" is still in use but is discouraged by Australian naturalists, since koalas are not related to the bears of America and Asia. —What is a koala and where does it fit into the marsupial pattern? Australia had marsupial carnivores, powerful creatures which dealt death as swiftly as any tiger or lion. Man, however, tends to look at death only as it affects him, and since there was no flesh-eater big enough to attack humans, a common mistake was that these marsupials were "gentle," that in this ark the equivalent of the lion lies down with the equivalent of the lamb. If this were true, it would fly in the face of all we know about animals, both past and present. Ever since life appeared there have been flesh-eaters to devour the plant-eaters. The Australian flesh-eating marsupials include the Tasmanian wolf, a marsupial as large as the wolf of other continents and big enough to kill a kangaroo or a sheep but shy of man. It was harried from the earliest days of white settlement because it could kill sheep, and today it is probably extinct.

15

Ranging down the size scale are the Tasmanian devils, snarling killers of small game; the native cats, the small dunnarts, and the tiny planigale, the size of a mouse; flesh-eaters all, though the flesh may be only a grasshopper.

The mark of all these carnivores is the fact that they have many and sharp teeth for killing and cutting up prey. A group called the bandicoots, named after a large rat of India and ratlike in general appearance, in many ways

A 58-day-old long-nosed bandicoot entering its mother's backward-opening pouch.

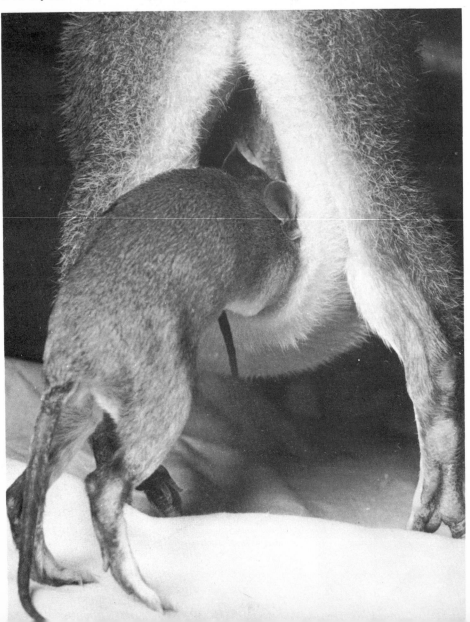

The first Australian marsupial to be seen by the European visitors was this species of tammar wallaby found on the Abrolhos Islands off the Western Australian coast where it is still common.

resembles the flesh-eating marsupials, since they have many teeth. They are also linked, however, with the herbivorous marsupials in that on the hind foot two of the toes are joined to make a fur comb. Scientists call this a syndactylous foot.

The herbivores are the largest and most spectacular of the marsupials and the ones best known to most people. They range in size from the giant kangaroos to the tiny honey possums. All belong to a group known as the diprotodonts. (This literally means "two front teeth" but should be read as "few," and refers only to teeth in the front of the jaw as there are more grinding teeth to the rear.) All have the syndactylous foot already mentioned, and

A brushtail possum. These marsupials share the gumtrees with the koalas and like them are mainly vegetarian.

The sugar glider possum lives in the treetops with the koalas. They cannot fly but are able to glide from tree to tree by spreading the skin flap that joins the hand and the ankle.

all have well-developed pouches. The kangaroos and wallabies form one large section of these plant-eaters, while the second is made up of an assortment—the possums, wombats, and the koala.

Where does the koala fit in in this family? Is it an oversized possum with the tail only a vestige, or is it closer to the wombat? There is one important difference from the possum in that the pouches of all the possum family open forward, and the koala mother has a pouch opening backward.

"Possum" is an Australian spelling to distinguish this marsupial from the American opossum. There is a great range in size in this group, from the tiny pygmy possum, weighing less than an ounce, to the koala, which can reach weights of more than thirty pounds. There is also a wide range of food preferences, with the smaller species varying the vegetarian diet with insects; some tap the sap of trees, relishing this sugary food material. Others eat fruit, leaves, and a variety of other plant parts, including the bark of trees.

The gliding marsupials also belong to this group. They have a fold of skin stretching from ankle to wrist which enables them to glide a hundred yards from one treetop to another tree trunk in the forest. Most of the family have a long prehensile tail and all have snug pouches, opening forward so that the baby when big enough stares out in the same direction as its parent.

The possumlike characteristics of the koala are the teeth, which resemble both those of the ringtail possum and the greater glider; the opposable thumbs, which are also possumlike; the leaf diet; and the tree-climbing habit.

There is one more group in the family—the wombats. Here we have a ground-dwelling animal as large as a koala, or larger, a burrower in the soil and, like the koala, with a pouch opening backward. For a burrower, a forward-opening pouch would present problems, since the baby would get a faceful of dirt every time the mother did a little digging.

Perhaps the koala, then, is a tree-climbing wombat? There are other parallels for ground-living marsupials taking to the trees in an apparent reversal of evolution. The rain-forest jungles of northeastern Australia are the home of tree kangaroos, very similar to ordinary kangaroos but with good climbing ability, though they look incongruous as they jump from branch to branch, or climb down a tree trunk, tail hanging toward the ground.

A scientific argument swayed around the koala for many years—wombat or possum?—until recently work on blood affinities by Dr. John Kirsch of Yale University threw more decisive light on the matter.

"Blood will out" is an old saying, which, Dr. Kirsch points out, is truer

The squirrel glider is slightly larger than a sugar glider but is similar in its habits.

The common wombat is considered the closest relative of the koala.

than we imagine. For many years scientists have been finding out relationships among animals by studying their blood. This is known as serology and is a study of antigens and antibodies and how they react. The antigens are usually proteins and consist of large molecules, which, when they invade another body, cause a reaction, and other large molecules known as antibodies are produced. These two terms have become familiar to us through a study of the diseases of man. As far back as 1904 it was suggested that this study could show relationships between animals.

Without going into the details of the techniques used, we can see the conclusions that Dr. Kirsch drew after studying the blood of marsupials, varying from the Virginia opossum to a large group of Australian marsupials.

The first interesting discovery was that every Australian marsupial studied is more closely related to the others than to the Virginia opossum. In the South American high Andes is a group of small marsupials, known as the caenolestids, which look something like shrews and have been thought to be possible ancestors of, or related to, the Australian diprotodonts. Serology came up with the answer that they are quite different from the Australian marsupials and just as different from the opossum. This indicates that evolution has been going on just as long in the marsupials of South America as in those of Australia.

The similarities between kangaroos, bandicoots, native cats, and the koala, however, showed that the wombat and the koala are the closest in terms of blood. The weight of evidence now suggests that the koala is really a tree-climbing wombat—or maybe the wombat is a ground-living koala!

3. A STEADY DIET OF GUM LEAVES

Now for a look at an adult koala. It has an appealing face, an impossibly large teddy-bear nose, small, sagacious eyes, and large ears. The fur is dense and woolly, gray above and lighter-colored below.

There is a difference in appearance between the koalas living in southern Australia and those in the north. A general rule with animals living over a wide range of latitudes is that the individuals living in the colder parts of the range are larger, and this is true of the koala. The koalas of the colder southern areas have shaggier coats and are more attractive in appearance than the smaller and browner northern forms.

The large pouch opens backward, and inside are two teats for the milk supply for the baby.

The forearms have three fingers separated from the other two, making the hand an efficient grasping and climbing organ. On the back legs the first toe is opposed to the others. The second and third toes are joined to make a comb for the fur, and the fourth and fifth are strongly clawed for climbing. The forearms and the legs are almost equal in size and are very powerful.

The neat arrangement of muscles and bones in arms and legs of all animals is a complicated system of levers which gives advantages in terms of large movements, strength, or flexibility. Professor W. A. Osborne records that the insertion of the powerful thigh muscle is very much lower on the shin in the koala than in other animals. This means that the koala sacrifices speed of movement for strength when climbing. "Slow but sure" is an important motto when a fall from a tree can mean injury or death.

Both front and hind limbs have granular pads on the underside of the

A typical koala face.

palms of the hands and the soles of the feet. These help in gripping a tree trunk and act as cushions when koalas take a flying leap through the air from one branch to crash-land on another. In this way their feet are similar to the possum's—also an adept climber and jumper.

The koala has a short, stumpy tail similar to that of the wombat. Since it spends many of the daylight hours comfortably wedged in a tree crotch, the lack of a tail suits the koala's resting habit.

The koala's head is large compared to the rest of the body, and the teeth are strong. The first pair of upper and lower incisors are large, long, and pointed, while the rest of the teeth are small and set well back. As a leaf-eating marsupial the koala has not only powerful jaw muscles and cutting teeth but cheek pouches which aid in food storage. An extraordinary feature of its anatomy is the appendix or cecum, which is two to three yards in length and is an aid in digesting leafy material.

This combination of strong feet for climbing and powerful jaws and teeth for eating the leaves of gum trees, as well as a strong heavy body that can reach a weight of more than thirty pounds, makes the koala a formidable animal. Enemies such as the dingo, powerful owl, or the goanna, though able to kill young animals, give mature koalas a wide berth.

A Victorian naturalist, B. E. Carthew, had an interesting story told him by a woodcutter. The man was working with a chain saw when he looked up and saw a large male koala advancing in menacing fashion. The animal grabbed him by the trousers and bit him on the leg and wrist when he struggled with it. Finally the woodcutter was able to overpower the koala and take it back into the bush. When it was placed in a box for removal, it kept up a very loud, growling cry.

The koala's call has been described as a harsh, grating sound, like a handsaw going through a thin board, so perhaps the explanation of this extraordinary attack is that the chain saw made the kind of noise characteristic of koalas fighting over territory. We know that for a robin redbreast even a patch of red feathers will bring an attack by a rival male bird. There could well have been some significant notes coming from the chain saw that were enough to set the koala into a territorial rage.

The solidity and strength of the koala was well demonstrated when one large male sat in the middle of a busy highway and refused to budge. A traffic jam occurred, until after about fifteen minutes the animal moved off into the bush.

Although the koala lives mainly high in the trees and prefers to move from treetop to treetop by means of interlacing upper branches, it can move

When the baby koala has grown large enough it leaves the pouch and travels on its mother's back, where the baby would be less likely to be bumped against branches.

fairly rapidly over the ground, running very much like a wombat. If pursued on the ground, as soon as it reaches the base of a tree, it will leap about a yard at the first jump, then make a series of upward jumps until it is high enough to avoid attack by the ground enemy. It then begins its hand-over-hand movement to reach a feeding or roosting place.

Koalas are strong swimmers, although fairly clumsy, moving along with almost all the body submerged. They are present on Magnetic Island, a few miles off the coast of Queensland near the port of Townsville, and local residents claim they have seen koalas swim ashore on this island, either coming across from the mainland or swimming across a bay rather than walking around on land.

A koala travels through the denser forests without having to go to the ground. Climbing to the outermost branch where its weight bends the branch until it touches the branches of a nearby tree, the koala can then move across to a new feeding tree.

Despite all this toughness, handlers of koalas in zoos say that their bodies are more delicate than is usually imagined. An animal should be lifted by gripping it around the waist or lifting it directly by means of the arms.

The gumtree is the trademark of the Australian bush, and it is appropriate that the koala should regard it as its favored food. This group of trees is uniquely Australian, native only to this continent and to some islands to the north.

The eucalypts, or gum trees as they are usually called, dominate 95 per cent of the Australian forests and can be found over practically all the continent except in the lush rain forests. There are more than five hundred species, ranging from those that live in the high country and are often covered with snow in the winter, such as the alpine gum, to those that thrive along water courses in the desert, such as the river red gum. It is one of

When in a hurry a koala can move up a tree in a series of jumps, gripping firmly with its long sharp claws after each leap.

the hardiest of all tree groups, and eucalypts are now being grown in about sixty countries around the world.

In height the eucalypts vary from the stunted mallee of about five feet to the mountain ash, the tallest hardwood tree in the world, which towers 385 feet in the air, overtopped only by the redwood tree of California, which reaches a majestic 440 feet. The redwood, however, is a softwood pine, so Australia can claim to have the world's tallest flowering plant.

Eucalypts belong to the myrtle family, and in Australia there are four important genera—Eucalyptus, Syncarpia, Angophora, and Tristania. All have stiff, harsh leaves able to remain rigid during times of drought, unlike the broad soft leaves of other plants, which wilt under such conditions.

The leaves of the myrtle family are rich in oil glands. If a gum leaf is held to the light, small translucent dots can be seen. These are the oil glands

scattered through the leathery leaves. In some species as much as one-twenty-fifth of the green weight of the leaf is oil, though in most it is only about one-hundredth. From the oil-rich gum trees eucalyptus oil was and still is distilled, possibly one of the first products to be exported from Australia and still used in most parts of the world.

The name "eucalyptus" means well covered and was given by botanists because in this particular genus the flowers have no petals, these having been fused into a cap which covers the developing stamens and other parts

of the flower. This cap falls away when the flower opens. The other name, "gum tree," arose from the fact that many kinds exude gum from wounds in the bark. This is not a gum in the strict sense but a kind used by the early aborigines as a medicine and today for tanning leather.

Koalas are very particular, both in the choice of leaves they eat on a particular tree and in the kind of tree they will use as a food supply. In some areas certain species are favored—for example, the manna gum in Victoria and the forest red gum in New South Wales. Through the years more and more plants that koalas eat have been discovered. At least fifty different species of eucalypts have already been listed as food, and this number is sure to be increased.

Koalas in different areas have different food preferences. In South Australia the koala was never widespread, being found only in the southeast corner. With white settlement, numbers diminished until recently, when new colonies were established in this state. The food trees include water gum, manna gum, and pink gum. On Kangaroo Island a naturalist observed an animal feeding on wattle, a species of acacia. These wattles are often used for shelter in hot weather, as they provide more shade than the sparser-leaved gum trees.

In Victoria the five most popular food trees are the manna gum, swamp gum, messmate, mountain gray gum, and the long-leaved box, which is also a eucalypt. The food list for this state includes twenty species, the high country snow gum being included. Some of these may be roosting trees rather than food trees, although koalas normally roost in their food trees. The manna gum is regarded as most popular with the koala, although in some areas colonies survive almost entirely on southern blue gum and in other places on black box. One animal was even seen eating the leaves of the introduced weeping willow.

In New South Wales more than twenty species of gum tree were found to be used as food, with the gray gum and forest red gum prime favorites.

In Queensland the food tree best liked by the koala is the forest red gum, and here again more than twenty different kinds of gum tree are used for food. A report from the Botanic Garden at Toowoomba in southern Queensland produced some surprising results. In the nearby bushland the favored tree was the broad-leaved box, but wild koalas visiting the gardens preferred to eat the ornamental eucalypts from Western Australia, a state where the koala is not found as a native. More than thirty species of eucalypt were eaten or slept in, but one Western Australian tree, the coral gum, was disliked enough to be avoided both as food and as a sleeping place. The

Behavior patterns vary and in captivity koalas often feed in the early afternoon.

developing buds of a callistemon, which produces bottlebrush-shaped flowers, was relished. In general, koalas seem to prefer trees with a large crown of leaves and a short trunk.

Various sanctuaries, such as Lone Pine in Queensland, have worked on the basis that each koala needs about a hundred food trees for its survival. In Victoria the stocking rate of forests was worked out at one animal to every two acres. A careful watch had to be kept in case some natural barrier concentrated animals more closely. Then they would eat themselves out of both house and home, since a food tree would become stripped bare and die.

Some surprising artificial diets have been recorded over the years. An early account from the 1930s tells of some pet koalas which had been fed

Rescued by a Melbourne doctor, a wild koala with a broken leg is given an anesthetic before the leg is set.

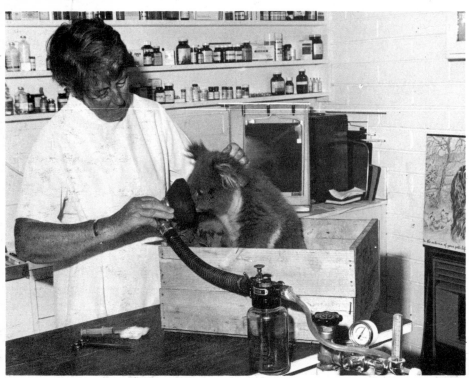

A gray kangaroo mother and her baby in the forest country, also the home of the koala.

The teddy-bear profile.

A baby koala peers uncertainly out of its mother's pouch, which opens backwards.

Tasmanian devil on the prowl. This marsupial carnivore is no longer a threat to the koala since it now lives only on the island of Tasmania.

A baby koala shelters from the rain, protected by the bulk of the mother's body, on Phillip Island.

A feathertail glider on a banksia blossom. This mouse-sized marsupial is a possum usually found over much the same range of forest country as the koala.

Koalas seen by day are usually asleep or moving very slowly, although when searching for food, climbing, or traveling toward another tree, they can move quickly.

A koala chewing contemplatively on a gumleaf.

A mother brushtail possum with her youngster. Like the koala, the baby possum when big enough leaves the pouch and rides on the mother's back.

A climbing koala.

A baby koala takes its first walk outside the pouch when it is about six months old.

A koala asleep wedges itself comfortably in a tree fork, where it is safe, no matter how much the tree moves in the wind. The long claws are separated into two groups of three and two fingers, enabling it to grip the tree trunk.

The golden possum of Tasmania is a color variety of the common brushtail possum. Both possums and koalas were hunted in earlier times for their attractive fur, but today with strict protection extinction has been avoided.

A baby koala poses for its portrait.

A powerful owl, a deadly enemy of the koala, perched in a tree in a eucalypt forest in Victoria.

The doctor's three young daughters fed "Koalie," meals of jam and biscuits, a most unusual diet for an animal which lives almost entirely on gumleaves.

on a mixture of bread and milk sprinkled with eucalyptus oil. The animals survived and were sleek and fat. Injured koalas being kept in homes while their wounds mended have developed a taste for jam.

An extraordinary story comes from the period of World War I. A soldier told how in 1915 a koala which was the mascot of his army unit was taken on the long sea journey to Egypt. It was kept alive on a diet of apples soaked in eucalyptus oil but was ill by the time they arrived in Egypt. It was saved by being fed leaves from roadside eucalypt trees, which are common in Egypt. The koala was given to the Cairo Zoo when the army unit sailed for Gallipoli.

A traditional pose of the koala is shown with the State's floral emblem of the red and green kangaroo paw in the foreground.

4. THE KOALA'S DAY

Vincent Serventy began his first studies of koalas in a roundabout way. Because he was born in Western Australia, the closest look he could get at koalas was through studying the fossil bones of the animals found in limestone caves in southwestern Australia. Then he had an opportunity to work in New South Wales on a film about koalas. This is his story:

My duties were many and varied. I was to act as koala catcher, animal trainer, platform builder, and anything else necessary to persuade the animals to follow the script. Of course, the script was fairly simple. Koalas had to climb up, climb down, look up, look down, go to the ground, and go up the trees again. To add a little difficulty, the baby had to climb up, climb down, look up, look down, go to the ground, and go up the tree again, and then climb over to the safety of the mother's back and head.

It all seemed delightfully simple on paper, but it wasn't quite so simple in practice. The koalas we met had a few major ideas—to eat, to sleep, and perchance to dream, although, to judge from the solidity of their sleeping poses, whatever dreams they had were tranquil ones.

Koalas are late risers and determined sleepers. Once a koala is solidly wedged into a tree crotch or an upper branch, the most vigorous shaking will do no more than cause it to lift its sleepy head, glance slowly toward the ground with slitlike eyes, and then drop its head to make the furry ball complete once more.

We shot a certain amount of film at Taronga Zoo in Sydney, particularly the pouch sequences. As the weather was cold, the baby showed no in-

A koala asleep in the shade on a hot summer day.

clination to leave the snug pouch. I tickled the youngster until we obtained a lot of film of kicking legs, and, once, an irritated-looking baby peering indignantly at the outside world before retreating.

We needed, however, a baby big enough to ride on the mother's back or head, and so we wandered, searching for one through the bush country north of Sydney. Though we located several koalas, we found only one baby of the right size, and as the koala and baby were about sixty feet above the ground in a tall gum tree, catching the pair was not easy.

Our technique was to lasso the adult to keep it from climbing any higher. The lasso was fastened loosely to a long, thin pole. The catcher, standing at the top of a long ladder, was able to drop the lasso neatly over the head of the koala. Sometimes we found a lasso was not needed, as pressing the head of the koala gently with the pole was enough to start it climbing down the tree trunk into our waiting arms. Though this sounds brutal in description, it was not so in practice. For many days I carried scars on my arms where the claws of one irate mother showed her displeasure at being captured.

The anxiety of the mother koala when she was separated from her baby was touching, and when for the purposes of filming I had to remove the youngster, she watched me with great distress until her baby was returned to her. When I put the baby on the ground, it would climb up my body, inflicting minor scratches all the way until finally it reached my head, dug its claws firmly into my rather plentiful hair, and triumphantly surveyed the world. The baby did not share the mother's obvious anxiety. Apparently any head was good enough as long as there was enough fur there.

Through the years I have watched koalas in the wild in numerous places, and I have seen that the shifting of the baby from the pouch to the back or head is an obvious advantage to the youngster. A mother may jump three or four feet from one branch to another, and when she lands with a thump, a baby in the pouch takes most of the punishment.

When shifting from one tree to another, the koala normally puts its weight on a branch until the branch leans across to engage with the branches of the next tree. Then the koala reaches across and moves to the next branch. In this case the baby has a smooth ride.

If trees are far apart, the animal makes a slow and careful backward descent until it reaches the ground and then runs rapidly to the nearest tree. A series of upward leaps brings it to safety.

High up again in the branches, the koala may begin to feed or decide to take a little nap. After sleeping steadily until ten in the morning, most of

53

A baby koala clinging to its mother's back for a comfortable ride.

A baby koala samples a gumleaf as a change from milk.

the animals in the sanctuary where we were filming would begin to feed. They took catnaps throughout the day and moved into fuller activity only in the early hours of darkness.

A feeding koala looks enchanting. It solemnly pulls a spray of leaves close and takes a sniff. Then the decision on flavor and texture has to be made. After the koala has rejected unsuitable leaves, the chosen ones disappear between its teeth as though they were shifted along an assembly

Baby koalas posed for the photograph are seen in groups only in captivity.

line. Sometimes all the labor of feeding becomes too much, and the animal falls asleep with a half-chewed leaf still gripped between its teeth like a smoker's pipe.

I envied the comfortable way a koala could settle into a tree crotch, while I perched precariously, trying to photograph the animals in an environment that was certainly not home to me.

Following a group of koalas in a farm paddock in northern New South

55

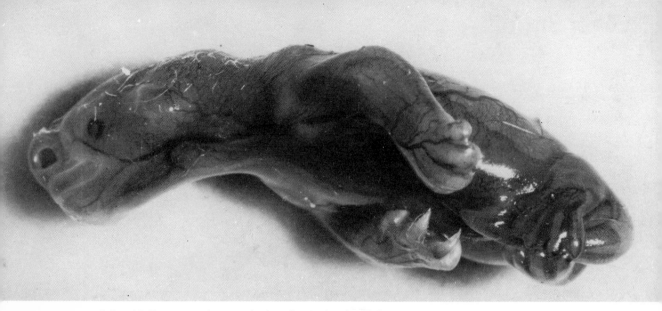

A brushtail possum photographed an hour after its birth.

A newborn brushtail possum, naked and blind, makes the perilous climb to the safety of the mother's pouch.

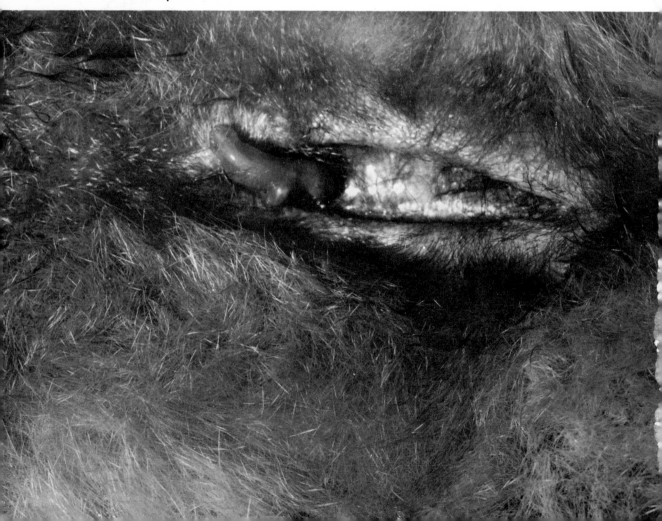

Wales showed me that, when necessary, the animals could cover long distances even when feeding. On Magnetic Island in north Queensland, Geoffrey d'Argieval, who runs a small sanctuary for koalas, found that one animal which was released some fifteen miles on the other side of the island, was back home two days later, demonstrating its homing ability and rapid rate of travel.

The usual impression of koalas, particularly of adult males, is that they are solitary creatures; however, recent research in Victoria shows that males have small harems of two or three females, which remain together in the mating season at least. At night in spring and summer most activity becomes apparent. The grating calls echo through the forest canopy as males fight to establish their harems. The loud calls possibly attract unmated females to a particular canopy territory. To our ears, the clamor is an angry sound, but to the listening female koala it may be a song of love.

The gestation period, as with most marsupials, is a short one, and some thirty-five days later the tiny baby koala is born. This fragment of flesh is less than three-eighths of an inch in length at birth and weighs about a fifth of an ounce—thus the embryonic nature of a marsupial baby such as the koala is obvious. Though single births are normal, there have been a number of reports of twins being found in the pouch.

Though the birth of a koala has not yet been described, it probably follows that of other marsupials. The tiny baby climbs steadily until it reaches the pouch, which has previously been licked clean by the mother. It fastens onto the teat so firmly that any attempt to pull it off will rupture the skin around the mouth and make it bleed. This bleeding led to the old bushman's legend that marsupial babies were actually born in the pouch budding off from the teat. With newly born kangaroos it is possible to manipulate the youngster gently off the teat and, after examination, replace it. The watching and finally the filming of marsupial birth in the kangaroo has at last destroyed this myth of pouch birth.

The baby gradually develops fur and leaves the pouch at the age of about six months. It remains with the parent for another six months and in captivity may stay even longer. Weaning is accomplished in an extraordinary manner, first observed by the Director of the Adelaide Zoo, Mr. Keith Minchin. The sheer bulk and fibrous nature of the gum leaves need the physiological aid of the huge appendix of the adult koala for digestion. The baby, after being fed on milk for six months, needs some graduated passage to the adult diet. Mr. Minchin found that when the baby is to be weaned, the adult passes out droppings of what seems to be partly digested food, and the baby eats them.

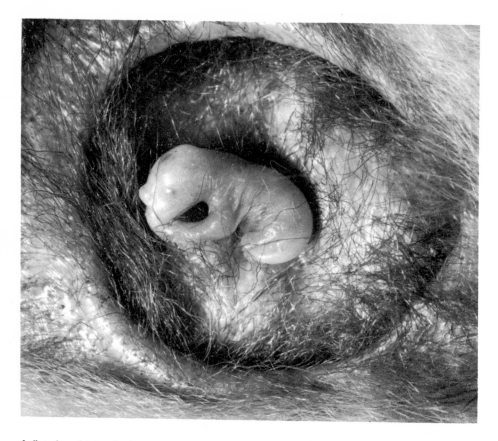

A five-day-old brushtail possum sucking milk from the teat in the mother's pouch.

For the next two months the baby uses the pouch for shelter and then takes to the mother's back or her head, depending on the circumstance of the ride. At one year of age it is able to become independent, and normally the yearling leaves the home range and spreads onto nearby areas, although in zoos it may stay longer with the mother and possibly inhibit her breeding the following year.

Females are mature when they are two years old, but the age of maturity of the male is not yet known. One captive specimen lived for twelve years, but possibly koalas may live to twenty years in the wild.

A distressed baby koala can make a cry extraordinarily like that of a human baby. We have heard it several times, and on the last occasion it was because we were trying to get a youngster which had become separated from its mother to move back toward the branch in which she was feeding. We had found that a way to stir any koala into activity was to make a scratching sound on the tree trunk. Perhaps this sound is a warning to a koala that a large and voracious tree goanna is on the prowl. These giant lizards would be quite capable of swallowing a young koala.

The dragging of a piece of dead timber down the trunk a few times stirs even the most somnolent koala into active climbing. This time we decided

A tammar wallaby mother with the pouch pulled open to show the tiny baby inside.

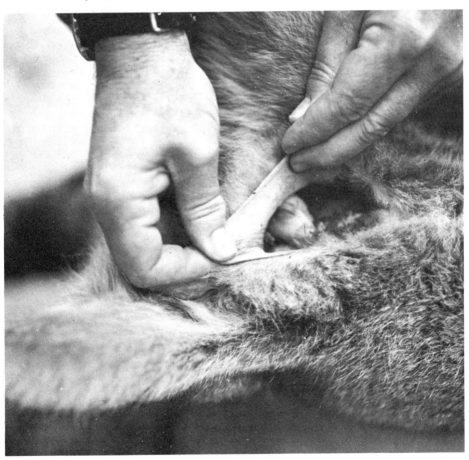

A baby koala enjoys a nap while hanging from its mother's pouch.

A baby koala having just left the pouch takes its first ride on its mother's back.

to try the technique with the baby, and the results were dramatic. The baby burst into a loud wail. We stopped scratching and retreated in some dismay. The baby kept on wailing. We moved a hundred yards off and the wail followed. We moved off a quarter of a mile. The heartbroken sobbing continued to echo through the bush, and it seemed that all the bush animals were looking at us indignantly.

It was in 1880 that the first animal was taken alive to Europe, where, zoologist Ellis Troughton says in *Furred Animals of Australia,* "it thrived under special care until in nightly wanderings it was caught in the lid of a fixed washstand and suffocated."

Mr. Troughton records a pet animal, reared from the age of three months, which became an exacting and not unintelligent pet. It was removed from its original home in Proserpine, Queensland, and fed on a diet of a quarter of a pint of cow's milk supplemented by blue gum leaves. Bags of fresh leaves were collected on the slow sea voyage around the south coast to Western Australia. It was fed here on leaves of local eucalypts, the York gum and the flooded gum with an additional half pint of milk and some peppermints. The koala was observed eating soil from time to time, possibly because of a mineral deficiency in its diet. Similar behavior has been reported of other koalas both in captivity and in the wild.

This question of mineral deficiency may explain why koalas feed on a particular species of tree in one part of their range, yet avoid the same species of tree growing in another part.

Noel Burnet, who established the Koala Park near Sydney, found that two Victorian koalas which he brought to his sanctuary refused to eat the local leaves on which the other koalas were thriving. For six months he had to have loads of manna gum leaves brought from the south, until finally the animals accepted the taste of the local plant. The average amount of food eaten was about two and a half pounds of leaves a day for each animal, so Mr. Burnet found feeding these two koalas an expensive proposition.

In carrying out research on the food needs of koalas, he found wide variations in the chemical content not only of different tree species but also in the variations produced by local soils. In general the koalas showed a preference for smooth-barked trees with high oil content.

Ambrose Pratt, a Victorian naturalist, had a number of tests carried out on gum leaves of various kinds, at different seasons and from different areas. A startling discovery was that the gum tips of young leaves at certain seasons could contain the deadly poison hydrocyanic acid, popularly known as prussic acid. Lambs have been killed by eating the young leaves of the sugar gum, and here the same poison was involved. The leaves of the manna gum, a favorite food tree of the koalas, are capable of yielding amounts of hydrocyanic acid dangerous to animals. There is probably a wide range of eucalypts in this class, but most research has been on shrubs that are eaten by stock. The taller gum trees may be dangerous to native animals such as koalas and possums, but only accidentally would they ever be eaten by sheep and cattle.

There is still a lot to be learned about the food needs of koalas, but certainly in some areas koalas can flourish even though they feed on only one kind of tree, so long as there is enough choice in the term of maturity in the leaves.

A koala looks at its reflection in a mirror. Naturalist Harry Frauca's experiments on the behavior of koalas noted that smell was used by the koala to recognize one another, but at close range sight became important.

5. SLAUGHTER AND NEAR EXTINCTION

Bones of the koala have been found as fossils in the southwest corner of Australia. The slow drying-out of the continent forced changes in habitat that killed off the koala in this area and reduced its range over the rest of Australia.

The coming of aboriginal man about thirty thousand years ago brought hunting pressure on the koala. Many a koala died to provide a tasty meal to be cooked over a campfire. The skins were not wasted; they were used for decorative belts.

The tree-climbing ability of the koala provided it with a measure of safety. Though aborigines were skilled climbers, a koala, by moving onto slender branches and then shifting to another tree, could avoid pursuit. Hunting spears, though ideal for killing ground game, were not effective when hurled upward. A well-aimed throwing stick might knock a sleeping koala off its perch, and possibly the koalas were forced into a nocturnal pattern of feeding to avoid being seen by the aborigines, who hunted only by day.

Some ten thousand years ago a new wave of aboriginal migrants brought with them their hunting ally, the wild dog, known today as the dingo, and a new hazard was added to any ground-moving koalas.

It has been claimed that the use of fire by the aborigines as a hunting tool was another factor in reducing the numbers of koalas. All the evidence points to the fact that the burning tended to keep the forest country open and clear of undergrowth. Most of the fires were lit in summer and would run slowly across the forest floor for months on end, dying away at times, then flaring up. This very light burn meant that the trees of the forest suffered a scorching at the base only, and this was no danger for the animals living in the forest trees. Perhaps it was even an advantage, as when the koala did descend to the ground the very open nature of the country would allow it to avoid attacks by ground hunters, such as the Tasmanian tiger and Tasmanian devil and later the dingo.

With the arrival of the first white settlers, the koala was common in the dry forest country from southeast of South Australia through Victoria and New South Wales into Queensland. Their numbers at the time must have been in the millions, and for about a hundred years the koalas entered a halcyon period. The aboriginal hunters were swept away by the white settlers in the all too common pattern of indigenous peoples around the world. Some aborigines were killed deliberately, some died of diease, but most, with their hunting grounds taken for farms, became hangers-on around white settlements, losing both the taste and skill for hunting native game. The clearing of the forests, however, meant that gradually the koala populations became less, for the ax always kills more surely than the gun. When the tree falls, so must the koala, because at one stroke it has lost food and home.

Mysterious crashes of the koala populations were reported between 1817 and 1819 and between 1900 and 1903. There is still argument as to the cause. Dr. Adolph Bolliger a bio-chemist, who worked in the Department of Surgery at the University of Sydney, examined a number of cases of diseased koalas and found that pneumonia was a common killer. The two population crashes recorded were said to be caused by ophthalmia and periostitis of the skull. In earlier times alarmists proclaimed that the koala was doomed because it was either genetically an unhealthy animal or it could not withstand diseases brought in with domestic stock, such as sheep and cattle. There have been dissenting voices among scientists, however, as to the extent of disease in these animals. Recent reports of individual animals dying from disease proved false upon investigation.

We can accept that there were rises and falls in the populations of koalas, as happens with many grazing and browsing animals.

The great decline and fall in the koala population cannot be excused by any special pleading of natural causes. It came from the greed of man when it was discovered that the fur of the koala was worth money.

The slaughter to near extinction began early in this century, and the numbers of koalas killed were staggering. In the year 1908, 57,933 skins were sold in the Sydney markets. Between 1920 and 1921, 205,679 koalas were killed for their fur, but by 1924 the killing had become a flood and two million skins were sent out from the eastern states.

By this time the tide of public opinion was forcing the hunters to market the skins under the name of wombat. Dealers hoped nobody would care if the wombats were destroyed, as they were regarded as a pest species. This is a curious parallel to the marketing of egret plumes under the name of osprey feathers, as, similarly, it was thought nobody would care if a mere fish hawk was destroyed.

The methods of killing the koala were barbaric. Naturalists A. S. Le Souef and Harry Burrell expressed the opinion, "Only the most callous of shooters can bring themselves to shoot such a childlike animal." The scientist Dr. Frederick Wood Jones wrote, "Indeed, one may say on humanitarian grounds, that not only should the slaughter of the Koala for the fur trade be prohibited because the animal is eminently one to protect and not to exterminate, but it should be prohibited because, like the slaying of seals, it is the most brutalising occupation that a human being can undertake."

Still the slaughter went on. The koalas of South Australia were wiped out. The numbers in Victoria fell so dramatically that in the 1920s one estimate put the total population at some 500, though this may have been an under-

This rare photograph of a live Tasmanian tiger was taken in Hobart Zoo, Tasmania about 1933. Fossil evidence indicates the tiger was on the mainland thousands of years ago, however when the first white settlers arrived in Australia, it was found only on Tasmania where it was hunted to near extinction because it killed sheep and lambs.

The dingo, a more serious enemy of a koala moving along the ground, arrived with the Aborigines about 8,000 years ago, and is now found on the Australian mainland.

estimation. The populations of New South Wales suffered a dramatic decline. Only in Queensland was there some hope for the future, since this state is so huge and its forests so vast that koalas were still common.

By this time the koala was legally protected in most states, but there was a serious problem. Even though a state such as Victoria had endeavored since the turn of the century to protect koalas legally, poachers still shot animals there and marketed the skins in a state which allowed this selling. Knowing that politicians come and politicians go, a shooter would continue to collect his skins and store them until the next open season. So long as there was the possibility of an open season, the slaughter went on, and koala numbers diminished everywhere.

By the mid 1920s so strong was public opinion against the trade that it seemed impossible that protection would ever be removed from the koala, but conservationists were soon to learn the bitter lesson that no fight is ever entirely won.

In Queensland large koala populations remained, even though departmental figures showed that a million koalas had been killed under license in 1919 and 1920. (There had been legal protection for a few years up to 1920.) The government, as a result of public pressure, brought in another

67

closed season. Naturalists and the public were happy that common sense had triumphed over greed.

In 1927 rumors spread of a new open season. Naturalist Alec Chisholm went to the Premier, Mr. Forgan Smith, and was promised personally that there would be no open season. But politicians' promises are written on the wind, and the open season was declared, in 1927, by the state government, against the advice of experts.

Ten thousand licenses were issued to trappers, and more than half a million skins were marketed within a few months; no doubt many of these had been killed illegally long before and stored.

Day by day the newspapers outlined the slaughter. This time the politicians had underestimated the public reaction, and there was such a storm of protest that the government, after some face-saving maneuvers, closed the season. It has never been opened again.

In *The Great Extermination* A. J. Marshall, the editor, wrote, "Why did the Government of the day permit this abominable business? Votes and money are the answer. Small landholders and farm workers wanted the money. And the government wanted their votes. Rural votes are often vital votes." Professor Marshall also points out that some of the kangaroo species today are facing the same kind of slaughter the koala faced more than a generation ago.

What was the result of this carnage of the 1920s? Queensland naturalist David Fleay, one of the most knowledgeable of the workers in the field of marsupials, was of the opinion that "the Queensland populations suffered a blow from which they never recovered. In the other States the koalas had become rarities."

A tree trunk deeply scored by the sharp claws of climbing koalas.

6. THE LONG ROAD BACK

Among the carnage there were hopeful signs. A few individuals, such as A. K. Minchin of the Koala Farm in South Australia, Noel Burnet of Koala Park in New South Wales, and C. A. M. Reid of Lone Pine Sanctuary in Queensland, proved that koalas could be bred in captivity. More importantly, by providing the general public with a chance to see live koalas at close quarters, they built a wide interest in the marsupials and an affection for them—an affection that later was to show at the polls.

More important from the long-term view of restoring koala populations was action by governments. In this area Victoria has the best record. In the 1920s official alarm at the fate of the koala was translated into action. At the time, the Fisheries and Game Department began the task of catching koalas on the mainland and stocking a number of offshore islands in the hope that at least the koala would not become extinct. It was hoped that populations to restock the mainland would develop. This work has been carried on by the renamed Fisheries and Wildlife Department.

Mr. J. C. McNally, who for a time was the Deputy Director of the Department and is now Director of the National Museum in Melbourne, Victoria, has given the most detailed statement on conservation work with koalas.

The first steps toward conservation in Victoria had been taken by private individuals at the turn of the century when koalas were taken across to Phillip Island and French Island in Westernport Bay. Between 1929 and 1933, 165 koalas had been released on Quail Island to form another colony, and later Phillip, Chicken, and Snake islands were colonized.

These island populations flourished but were forgotten by officialdom

69

(overleaf)

A herd of gray kangaroos on the move across an open area in a sanctuary. Increased protection for Australian marsupials has resulted in many species gaining in numbers.

An appealing trio at Lone Pine in Queensland.

until local naturalists stirred the authorities into action. It was known that on these islands populations of koalas could build up rapidly, and, free from natural controls, be in danger of eating themselves out of house and home. Alec Chisholm and David Fleay, hearing alarming stories of the conditions of the koalas on Quail Island, went there in 1943. They found many dead trees and sixty dead koalas at all stages of growth, from young animals to mature adults. The government dismissed the report as alarmist, but later admitted that three-quarters of the one thousand koalas on the island were in danger. Action was taken to remove most of the animals to suitable areas on the mainland. After this salutary lesson the state authorities began to

Hanging on means the difference between life and death for a koala. A fall from a gumtree can result in an injury which almost always leads to death.

exercise more supervision of the populations on the islands, and the management program improved considerably.

Mr. McNally published in 1957 the results of a field survey carried out on French Island. This island is about forty thousand acres in size. The first koalas were taken there early in the century, and numbers built up rapidly, the koalas feeding on manna gums. Some estimates put populations as high as five thousand within twenty years. There was at least one population crash, and at the time of Mr. McNally's visit there were only between eight hundred and a thousand animals.

There were a number of farms on the island, and the farmers reported that the koalas tended to concentrate in small stands of manna gums until they defoliated them, and the trees would then die. The problem was no doubt accentuated by the clearing of forests for farms and the killing of

predators, such as wedgetail eagles, which might have kept the koala population in check.

As the island was overpopulated, it was decided to remove a large number of the animals to the mainland. These were caught by using the pole and lasso method with the addition of catching nets to cushion the fall of koalas which dropped to the ground. Measurements made on the 694 animals collected provided a wealth of information. Most of the animals were in excellent condition with no trace of disease. The total of 694 consisted of 245 males, 278 females, and 171 young still dependent on their mothers. One mother was seen with two youngsters on her back, but one of these may have been adopted after having been deserted by its own mother.

The weights of 523 of the koalas ranged from seven to thirty-two pounds, with females averaging seventeen and a half pounds and males twenty-one pounds. The size of the various young indicates that breeding took place from spring through summer.

About six years after this field survey, Mr. McNally published another paper summarizing koala management in Victoria. After pointing out that the offshore island sanctuaries are inspected regularly and surplus animals removed, he listed the requirements of a mainland area suitable for releasing koalas from the islands. The area must be large and have plenty of suitable food trees. It must also be safe in terms of its reservation, either as a national park, nature reserve, or state forest, and the fire risk must be low. Early accounts indicating areas that were once rich in koalas were good evidence that such areas are suitable for present-day release. Since this work began, seven thousand koalas have been used to restock more than fifty areas.

It has been found that adults must be crated separately, as males, particularly, are aggressive. Male and female young or a female with her youngster can be crated together.

The two islands, Phillip and French, provide the best success stories in terms not only of saving koalas but of allowing visitors to enjoy seeing the animals in the wild. There is not a great deal gained if an animal survives but becomes visually extinct, never to be seen by the average visitor unless trapped and held in a zoo. Seeing a koala in the best zoo is a poor substitute for seeing a koala in its native gum tree.

The koalas on Phillip Island thrive under the watchful eye of local committees who not only protect them but see to the planting of suitable food trees. Today this island is the best place in Australia to see koalas in a natural setting.

An alert koala looking for a new tree to visit

The major problem is the bush fire. The Director of the Department of Fisheries and Game, Mr. F. Lewis, has reported that after a fire swept through the manna gum colonies, the first new shoots were eagerly sought by the hungry survivors. These shoots have the highest concentration of prussic acid, possibly a natural device in the plant to protect the important growing tips from being eaten by animals. Normally the koala could avoid these tender leaves, possibly being warned by the taste, but under the spur of intense hunger such caution was forgotten.

Mr. Lewis also stated that in earlier years, with no surface water on the island, during long, dry summers some koalas would go down to the sea to drink salt water, usually with fatal results.

During World War II the tree-planting program suffered a setback, since so much timber was needed to fire the kilns which produced chicory. The cutting of the forests reduced the island potential as koala territory, but since then many new plantations have been established.

The koala population is carefully managed to make sure there are never too many animals. Surplus population is removed to the mainland, and the rest roam freely.

It is sheer delight to drive along the island roads, then suddenly become aware that the forest surrounding you is full of koalas. You can walk through leafy glades and at one point stop to admire a mother with her baby riding piggyback, at another see a huge male imperiously surveying his territory, or another fast asleep in a tree crotch. Some will be seen walking along horizontal limbs, while others sample gum leaves in a fastidious manner. At night the activity increases, and the air may be filled with the grating calls.

Phillip Island has delights other than the koalas. During the spring and summer months there is a wonderful penguin parade when tens of thousands of penguins come ashore to visit their nesting burrows.

Mention has been made of Keith Minchin and his work with koalas and their conservation. It was his idea to start a colony on Kangaroo Island off the coast of South Australia. A sanctuary here would be free of foxes and more easily protected from illegal shooters than mainland areas. An area of 212 square miles of the western end of the island was set aside, and in 1924 koalas were brought to a small enclosure where for seven years they fed on water gum leaves. They bred successfully, but, as in other smaller areas, they ate out the trees and were released into the nearby bush. Today they number many hundreds and live in the forest country along the river flats, their main food being manna gum, pink gum, and water gum. Mervinia Masterman studied this colony for a number of years and gives a fascinating picture of them in her book *Flinders Chase.*

She says that the main call appeared to be a kind of grunting snore, but she also has heard two koalas "talking to each other with a low crooning, almost a purring note." During the mating season many calls are heard at night.

One of the most heartening aspects of nature conservation in Australia is the way children have been in the forefront of the movement. When the governments became involved in koala management, children also wanted to help.

One successful project increased the numbers of food trees. In the late 1930s seeds of the manna, swamp, red, and river gums and the long-leaved box were supplied to any school willing to grow them as seedlings and transplant the young plants to suitable areas. Scout and Guide groups created small plantations of such trees.

This work was not confined to Victoria but spread into New South Wales. Tucki, near Lismore, was one such place where food trees were planted to ensure the survival of the small colony of koalas in this area. This work has continued to the present day and, it is hoped, will finally bring back koalas to most of the forests of eastern Australia.

During the past few years there have been mass surveys carried out by schoolchildren and analyzed by conservationists of the fortunes of the koala in the three major states, Victoria, New South Wales, and Queensland.

A previous census, taken in Victoria in 1941, revealed between seven hundred and eight hundred animals on Phillip Island and a few hundred more on other islands and the mainland. The total was placed at eleven hundred individuals, but as we have seen from overlooked islands, such as Quail Island, this was an underestimate. The total population may well have been ten times that. The same census indicated that it was difficult to get reliable information from the other states, but the general conclusion was that their populations were of somewhat the same order, although more scattered.

The children's recent census in Victoria gave heartening figures of more than fifty thousand animals, a tribute to the efforts conservationists have exerted to save the koala.

The National Parks and Wildlife Service of the New South Wales annual report of 1972 indicated that the animal, though widespread, is declining in numbers. Most of the population is now found in the Collarenebri–Lightning Ridge area and on the north coast. Surprisingly, some are still

living in the western plains, and small concentrations occur in the eastern and central divisions of the state. At the Narrandera Nature Reserve an area has been fenced and will be used as a breeding center.

The biggest single factor controlling the numbers of koalas seems to be the increased number of bush fires in New South Wales.

And what of Queensland, the stronghold of the koala? A survey carried out in 1967 was summarized by Dr. Jiro Kikkawa and Margaret Walter of the University of Queensland. Their conclusion was that the stronghold of the koalas is in the southeast corner and that most of the sightings occurred in the range of the common food tree, the forest red gum. Since the western limit of this particular tree roughly cuts the state in half from north to south, the bulk of the koala population lies to the east of this line.

Magnetic Island still remains the northernmost outpost, but the weight of opinion is that koalas were taken to this island and did not occur there naturally.

The survey showed that numbers are still low compared to the days before the 1927 slaughter, and there has been some shrinking of range since the killing stopped. There are still plenty of suitable habitats left for colonization, or recolonization, provided bush fires are controlled.

Last thoughts:

So it seems as though our koala story had the traditional happily-ever-after ending. Man will never deliberately cause another mass slaughter of koalas. There are, of course, the secret killers described in Rachel Carson's *Silent Spring.* Pesticides such as DDT find their way into penguins in far-off Antarctica and can just as easily find their way into the koalas in their gum trees. Yet today most governments are aware of the dangers of these lingering killers, and the persistent killers are being phased out.

Clearing of forests for lumber and for farms is a major threat. Australia still has less than 2 per cent of its various habitats set aside as national parks and nature reserves, so there is still a long way to go by world standards.

"Preserve the habitat and you preserve the animal" is the basic principle for the safety of koalas. Once the national park has been set aside, the next step is to solve the fire problem, since those furry bundles high up in a tree are safe from every danger except the flames of a flaring wildfire.

There is one last shot in the locker of conservation which has worked suc-

anxious mother hurries over the ground in search of a tree trunk and safety from an
tacking dingo or another ground enemy.

cessfully with some species: the sending of small stocks of animals to zoos and other reserves around the world so that, if disaster befalls an animal in its own country, at least it has not disappeared from the earth. Sir Peter Scott and his wildfowl sanctuary at Slimbridge in Great Britain have had marked success with breeding the Hawaiian nene geese.

However, there has been some opposition in Australia to the export of live koalas. In 1959 when plans were made to send a small colony to America, some conservationists strongly opposed the move. The koalas were sent and the colony still survives at the San Diego Zoo. There are ten animals—four males and six females—in the present colony. Until a larger sanctuary is provided in the more open type of zoo on the outskirts of San Diego, there seems no point in sending more animals to that particular place.

The few animals released on the islands off the Victorian coast soon grew into large colonies of several thousand. There is no reason that the same could not happen in any part of the world where suitable gum trees have been grown ready to house such a colony.

It is wise not to have all one's eggs in one basket, and the more countries that establish large sanctuaries for threatened animals the better.

A side benefit is that a visitor who sees kangaroos or koalas in a zoo usually wants to see such animals in their native home. A United States survey team hired as consultants by an Australian travel association produced a report commenting that the "koala is a tourist asset worth millions."

Many of us believe the world's future is bound up with people getting to know one another, not only through newspapers and movies but through personal contact. Tourism could well be a passport to world peace. If the koala attracts more people to visit Australia, it will be better for all of us—humans and koalas.